Roman Gardens

Roman Gardens

Anne Jennings

ENGLISH HERITAGE

IN ASSOCIATION WITH THE MUSEUM OF GARDEN HISTORY

Front cover: **Fresco of an ornamental garden from the empress Livia's villa at Prima Porta near Rome**

Back cover: **Fresco of a bird eating fruit from the Villa of Poppaea at Oplontis**

Published by English Heritage, 23 Savile Row, London W1S 2ET
in association with the Museum of Garden History, Lambeth Palace Road,
London SE1 7LB

First published 2006

ISBN-10 1 85074 935 3
ISBN-13 978 1 85074 935 6
Product code 50998

A CIP catalogue for this book is available from the British Library

Edited and brought to press by René Rodgers
Designed by Michael McMann
Technical editor Rowan Blaik
Printed by Bath Press

CONTENTS

Introduction

This book explores garden development during the Roman period, when ornamental horticulture was first practised in Britain. After their invasion of Britain in the 1st century AD, the Romans were keen to establish the lifestyles and culture they had left behind and some natives wanted to emulate them. Towns, villas and farmhouses, similar in style to those created in Italy, were built and these sometimes incorporated a key characteristic of Roman domestic architecture: the courtyard garden. Enclosed by the wings of the house, courtyard gardens created a private space for socialising and relaxation, and despite an unfavourable climate, similar gardens were made in Britain.

Roman influence can be seen in British gardens today. We still grow many plants that were introduced by the Romans and the formal training of fruit trees into cordons and espaliers can be traced back to their gardens. Indeed, the character and ambience of a courtyard garden today often bears many similarities to Roman creations, such as paved surfaces, plants in containers and formal pools.

Throughout this book, a number of practical 'how-to' sections provide tips on creating Roman-style features in your own garden and the lists of plants and trees available to gardeners from this period will help to evoke an authentic feel. The lists also give the availability of these plants, both as seeds and container-grown stock, in UK nurseries.

Espaliered fruit trees were popular in Roman gardens

Iron Age Britain (800 BC–AD 43) was quite densely populated and divided into different tribal territories. People generally lived in small farming settlements or occasionally in larger groups within fortified enclosures known as hillforts and pre-Roman towns, which Julius Caesar called *oppida*. By this time, much of the woodland in Britain had been cleared and Iron Age farmers practised mixed agriculture that included the cultivation of wheat and barley, and the rearing of cattle and sheep. From c 100 BC more intensive agricultural practices were used and technical innovations were being introduced. There is evidence that land that was more difficult to farm – such as floodplains, uplands and wetlands – was being cultivated and that field drainage was developed to improve productivity. Iron Age farmers were efficient and it is thought that they were producing surpluses. Indeed, Strabo (c 64 BC–AD 24), a historian and geographer, writes about the export of grain, cattle, hides, hunting dogs and slaves from Iron Age Britain to the Continent.

While the pre-Roman economy in Britain was primarily agricultural, Iron Age inhabitants were also skilled craftspeople who produced metalwork and pottery. They made ornate jewellery, clothes, tools and weapons from a variety of materials. Though there is no evidence of ornamental gardening in Britain before or during the Iron Age, many early agricultural tools were later adapted to horticultural use.

The Iron Age hillfort at Maiden Castle

Opposite: **A floral motif from a mosaic at Fishbourne Roman Palace**

The people, landscape and weather of this northern island held little attraction for the rulers of the Roman Empire. Nevertheless, mineral wealth and the desire to expand their empire meant that it was only a matter of time before the Romans invaded Britain. Following Julius Caesar's failed attempts in 55 and 54 BC, the island was finally conquered in AD 43 under the Emperor Claudius. Once Roman rule was established in the province, a different order and culture was introduced to Britain, together with a more sophisticated farming system that was often based around a large villa. The Romans also brought architectural and building skills as well as administrative organisation and greater access to international trade throughout their burgeoning empire.

Most of the population of early Roman Britain still lived in the country, but urban communities began to develop, gradually increasing in size and population. The forum and basilica formed the centre of the Roman town and served as a market and administrative space. Temples to a variety of gods were often found in other areas of the town. More rarely in Britain public bathhouses, amphitheatres and theatres were also provided. All of these elements served to form the civic, religious and social foci of a Roman town. Archaeological remains at Silchester in Hampshire show the layout of such a settlement, with a grid-like road system, a 'high street' where traders sold their goods from individual shops, a forum area

in the centre of the town and an amphitheatre outside the
city walls. By the 4th century AD Romano-British towns had
become more substantial, with stone and brick replacing
timber, and trade and commerce became increasingly
important aspects of urban life.

*A reconstruction drawing of the Roman town of Silchester
by Ivan Lapper*

Most Romano-British towns were not densely occupied, especially during the late Roman period, and there would have been considerable space for garden areas. The majority of town dwellers lived in small strip buildings on the street fronts or in more substantial townhouses. Many dwellings had gardens or plots attached where edible and medicinal plants such as lettuce, cabbage, poppies, pot marigolds and herb Robert could be grown. Water was usually carried to the home in buckets from a public fountain served by an aqueduct or drawn from a well, though it was sometimes piped in.

It is estimated that over 90 per cent of the population of early Roman Britain lived in the country and many still lived in Iron Age roundhouses. Early farmhouses were substantial, if relatively basic buildings, but from the end of the 1st century AD, Roman influence increased and its culture became more integrated into British life. At this time Roman-inspired villas began to appear, primarily in the southern areas of Britain, while in the north agricultural activity still concentrated on native farmsteads. Villas formed the hub of large agricultural estates and, though many were owned by farmers or run by their agents, some served as the country houses of people in high positions in the administration of the Roman province. Romano-British villas were generally quite different from those in central Italy and were typically made up of domestic and subsidiary buildings situated around a large open courtyard, or courtyards. The houses usually comprised long, narrow rooms, rather than being organised around an atrium or peristyle as is seen in villas from Italy and other parts of the empire (see p 22).

Some Romano-British villas were more architecturally elaborate, especially during the 3rd and 4th centuries, with bathhouses, dining rooms and reception areas being built. Sophisticated under-floor heating systems called hypocausts

A hypocaust at Fishbourne Roman Palace

Detail of the dining room mosaic at Lullingstone showing the abduction of Europa by Jupiter disguised as a bull

often added to the owners' comfort and interiors could be richly decorated, with marble surfaces, brightly coloured, painted and patterned walls and intricately detailed floors laid with bricks, tiles or mosaics. Mosaics were a particularly popular form of embellishment, with designs primarily derived from geometric patterns and mythological subjects, and fine examples have been found at the villa at Lullingstone in Kent. Here, a bathhouse that included hot, cold and warm baths was added to the villa in the later 2nd century AD and the dining room was expanded in the early 4th century AD and elaborated with an intricate mosaic depicting mythological scenes.

There is substantial surviving evidence of the Roman occupation and influence in Britain, including excavated remains in cities such as Bath, York and Colchester. The long, straight roads that cross the country and the remnants of city walls and Hadrian's Wall show the physical extent of their 350-year rule. The impact of Roman culture is evident in many ways: for example our alphabet, language and calendar have Latin roots. There is, however, only limited evidence for Roman gardens and horticulture in Britain and, apart from a few examples, we must look to other parts of the empire for clues to the appearance of these gardens and their translation into the English landscape and climate.

The Roman domination of Europe, Asia Minor and North Africa, with an empire that by AD 114 stretched from Britain to the Sahara Desert and across to the Red Sea, remains an awesome achievement in European history. From a small community living in wooden huts around 750 BC, Rome made a strategic and determined effort to invade and rule surrounding land. By 300 BC Rome controlled a large part of what was to become Italy and, over the next 100 years, the Roman army developed sailing skills that facilitated the conquest of lands in the wider Mediterranean region, including Spain and Egypt. Rome eventually defeated the Greek armies and Greece was incorporated into the growing empire by 146 BC. Greek culture proved to be a dominant force in Roman life and exerted a strong and permanent influence on the Romans and their empire. Similarly, the ancient cultures of Egypt, under Roman rule from 30 BC, and Persia (modern-day Iran), with whom a treaty was signed in 20 BC, also influenced Roman culture and garden-making.

Ancient Greece

The ancient Greeks were more plantsmen than garden designers. The topography of their country and a shortage of fresh water did not lend itself to extensive garden-making, though sacred sites, burial grounds, public spaces and palaces were often decorated with planting. Trees, plants and flowers

Bear's breeches, Acanthus mollis

11

were used for symbolic and aesthetic purposes and some had particular religious significance. Indeed, various plants were associated with specific gods and goddesses, and trees and other plants were often grown around Greek sanctuaries. Despite this, there is little evidence of early ornamental gardens of the type that are later seen in the Roman period. Instead, most gardens tended to be utilitarian market gardens, situated outside the cities to take advantage of nearby water sources, while farms in the surrounding countryside had orchards, agricultural fields and vineyards.

However, the Greeks knew a great deal about the richness of their native flora and these featured in ancient legends. Greek mythology tells us that the god Apollo fell in love with the water nymph Daphne after being shot by one of Cupid's arrows. Unfortunately, Daphne did not reciprocate his feelings and fled from him in terror. When it became clear that she could not escape Apollo's clutches she appealed to the river god to save her and he transformed her into a bay laurel tree. From then on, Apollo declared the laurel sacred to him and it was associated with his worship. Homer (c 745–700 BC), who Pliny the Elder referred to as the Greek 'father and prince of all learning', also made reference to horticulture and plants in his epic poems *The Iliad* and *The Odyssey*. For example Book VII of *The Odyssey* describes Odysseus's visit to the palace and garden of the Phaeacian king, which included an orchard with fruit trees, a vineyard and various garden beds. *The Odyssey* also refers to specific plants:

A 17th-century sculptural representation of the Apollo and Daphne myth by Bernini

> *With this the Slayer of Argus pulled the herb*
> *from the ground, and gave it to me, pointing out*
> *its features. It was black at the root with a milk-*
> *white flower. Moly the gods call it, difficult for*
> *mortals to uproot, though the gods of course can*
> *do anything.*

The Odyssey, Book X

The natural world also influenced architectural embellishment. For example, the carving of acanthus leaves on the top of Corinthian columns was supposedly inspired by a Greek legend. After a young Corinthian damsel fell ill and died, her nurse gathered the girl's trinkets and ornaments into a basket, to be set down near her young mistress's tomb. She unknowingly placed it over the roots of a dormant acanthus and, to prevent the contents being damaged by bad weather, covered the basket with a tile. In spring the acanthus leaves and stalks burst forth and spread themselves around the outside of the basket, bending back again where they touched the overlapping tile. A sculptor named Callimachus passed by and was so charmed by the beauty and novelty of this accident that he perpetuated the arrangement in stone.

Corinthian columns, decorated with the acanthus motif, are also found in Roman architecture. This intricate capital is from Pompeii.

However, it was the Greek landscape and flora, more than ideas about garden design, that had a real impact on Roman gardens. For example the Emperor Hadrian looked to Greece when creating his extravagant garden at Tivoli in the 2nd century AD, where he attempted to recreate a landscape similar to Thessaly in northern Greece (see pp 40–1). In later horticultural history, the natural landscape of Greece was also to be a great inspiration to 17th-century European landscape artists whose work in turn influenced the 18th-century landscape movement.

Egyptian gardens

The creation of ornamental gardens in Egypt would not have been possible without the River Nile, which flows through that arid country en route to the Mediterranean. Throughout history the Nile has brought life to the desert and, through its annual flooding, has created a strip of fertile soil along its margins. Its water has been diverted to irrigate crops growing on surrounding land, and in the same way water was brought into Egyptian gardens, the earliest of which can be traced as far back as 2000 BC. Water was stored in the garden in pools, canals and moat-like dykes, then carried or channelled through the site to water the plants.

Ancient Egyptians believed that the gods ruled their lives and honoured them by offering cut flowers in temple ceremonies. Sculptural representations of the gods were placed in Egyptian gardens and these, together with architectural features such as columns and pavilions, created a formal character. This formality was often emphasised by the way plants were used and cultivated, with sophisticated but practical horticultural techniques creating aesthetically pleasing effects. Grape vines would, for example, be pruned and trained into beautiful shapes to control vigour and increase cropping, and date palms were planted in long straight avenues for ease of watering from irrigation canals, at the same time creating formal axes with end focal points.

Egyptian floral ornament and motifs from Owen Jones's The Grammar of Ornament *(1856)*

It is easy to understand why, in the hot arid climate of North Africa, gardens became representations of paradise on earth. These enclosed havens where water and greenery dominated must have created a sharp contrast with the baking heat of the near desert conditions beyond. Tomb paintings have been found that show images of gardens planted with palms and lotus flowers around pools filled with fish. Other ancient Egyptian art depicts gardens planted with pomegranates, figs, myrrh trees and formally laid out orchards. All these images, whether actual or idealised, suggest a desire to create an earthly paradise that was to be a constant inspiration for garden-making throughout the centuries to come.

Persian gardens

In Persia, ornamental gardening was practised from around the 6th century BC, when once again the idea of an earthly paradise was the inspiration for garden-making. The earliest recorded Persian garden was made at Pasargadae, the capital of the Achaemenid empire, in Iran. This city was established by Cyrus the Great around 550 BC and resembled a large park with a citadel overlooking a garden and palace complex. The garden contained many of the elements that would become familiar in ancient and Roman gardens: rills, formal architecture, shaded pavilions, avenues of trees and irrigated planting beds. It is thought that pomegranates, almonds, vines and roses grew here, with cypress trees providing shade and structure.

Early Persian gardens were beautiful places that pleased the mind with their order and satisfied all the senses. Enclosure, symmetry and geometry underpinned the basic design and formed a backdrop to the more sensual elements: beautiful, perfumed plants, moving water, edible fruits and a myriad of textures. These were sophisticated gardens that can still teach us a great deal about the art and craft of garden-making on every level.

Despite the seemingly inhospitable climate, Persia had a rich and diverse natural flora that included now familiar bulbs such as tulips and grape hyacinth. Within the enclosed spaces of the early Persian gardens, protected from drying winds, plants could be cultivated and irrigated so that the reality of an earthly paradise would have been successfully achieved.

These early horticultural activities combined a need for practicality with a desire for beauty. The resulting gardens would inspire an emphasis on religious symbolism in later centuries – for example 7th-century Muslims related the formal, geometric designs of early Persian gardens to the teachings of the Quran with water symbolising one of the rivers of life. The number four had spiritual significance and the Persian technique of dividing a garden into quarters (a quadripartite design) using narrow canals or rills would later become a crucial element of Islamic garden design and layout.

The Generalife Palace in Granada, Spain, has a replanted Islamic garden based on a quadripartite design

Said to be one of the Seven Wonders of the Ancient World, the Hanging Gardens of Babylon were supposedly created around 600 BC on the banks of the River Euphrates. Though there is some dispute about the actual site and detail of the garden, the legend that has developed around it suggests a remarkable piece of engineering and horticultural design.

It is said that the garden was made for the wife of King Nebuchadnezzar II (reigned 605–562 BC), in an effort to recreate some of the beauty of Media (Kurdistan), the mountainous northern homeland for which she pined. It consisted of a series of dramatic planted terraces, steps and arches built of stone and irrigated by a system of pumps that drew water from the river. The terraces and voids between the brickwork were immense to allow the importation of enormous amounts of soil so that trees could be planted on the different levels. Contemporary writing suggests that the garden was rectangular and measured almost 500 metres in length and that it was tiered like the seats in a theatre. The main garden on the top level was effectively an early form of a roof garden.

Archaeologists are still trying to ascertain whether the gardens really existed, though literary evidence from both Greek and Roman authors certainly refers to a great garden made by the king and describes some of its features:

> [The garden] consists of vaulted terraces raised one above another, and resting upon cube-shaped pillars. These are hollow and filled with earth to allow trees of the largest size to be planted. The pillars, the vaults, and terraces are constructed of baked brick and asphalt.
>
> Strabo, c 64 BC–AD 24

> The Approach to the Garden sloped like a hillside and the several parts of the structure rose from one another tier on tier ... On all this, the earth had been piled ... and was thickly planted with trees of every kind that, by their great size and other charm, gave pleasure to the beholder ... The water machines [raised] the water in great abundance from the river, although no-one could see it.
>
> Diodorus Siculus, 1st century BC

An artist's impression of the Hanging Gardens of Babylon in Wonders of the Past (early 20th century)

Roman garden design in Italy

As Rome became ever more confident in its expanding empire and grew wealthier from the taxes paid by the lands under its rule, those in power created extravagant homes in which to socialise and entertain. Crucial to the Mediterranean lifestyle, then as now, was a direct relationship between the inside and the outside: the stone and marble decorated townhouse or villa provided a cool environment in which to escape the heat of the midday sun, while the enclosed courtyard created a retreat for both privacy and socialising in the gentler heat of the morning and evening.

Gardens belonging to the poorer members of Roman society were little more than small working plots providing essential edible and medicinal plants, but as the wealthy built ever larger and more extravagant homes, the surrounding outdoor space becoming increasingly sophisticated. From around 150 BC wealthy Romans were enjoying beautiful gardens that enhanced their lifestyles and by the start of the first millennium, an ornamental garden had become the 'must-have' accessory for anyone of standing within the Roman community, the grandest often being created for whichever emperor was in power at the time.

Whether in town or country, Roman gardens generally followed similar design theories and planting styles, though scale and setting varied enormously. Before considering the

> *First for the varied garden let rich soil, A place provide, which shows a crumbling glebe, And loosened clods, and, dug, is like thin sand.*
>
> De Re Rustica, Columella, 1st century AD

Detail of a garden painting from the House of the Golden Bracelet in Pompeii

different types of gardens, it is useful to understand the basic style of Roman houses and gardens in Italy in order to better appreciate how they were translated into different environments.

Traditionally an atrium was located inside the entrance to a Roman house. This space was often highly decorated and had an *impluvium*, or pool, to collect rainwater through an opening in the atrium roof. Some atriums in Pompeii and Herculaneum were also treated as small decorative spaces with planted containers placed around the central pool. Houses were usually designed around a central courtyard or peristyle that was open to the sky with a portico, or covered walkway supported by columns, running around this central space. A separate pool or fountain would often form the central focal point within the courtyard and the remaining space would be paved with stone, tiles, bricks and mosaics or, in more utilitarian gardens, compacted earth or sand. Box plants often formed decorative hedges that defined or delineated the space, and pots, statues and other features, including topiary, were placed symmetrically around the paved courtyard.

The most striking feature of many Roman gardens, and one that demonstrates influence from early Egyptian and Persian gardens, was their formal layout based on geometric patterns. Roman gardens were principally architectural creations,

dominated by the structure of the townhouse or villa and 'hard' elements in the garden such as paths and walls. These straight boundaries imposed a formal layout on the site. Other practical requirements, such as the laying of pipes or digging of small canals to carry water, and a grid-like system of paths for easy cultivation and harvesting of beds, would also have dictated straight lines. These in turn created small vistas, at the end of which a focal feature would be placed.

These gardens were often used as social spaces and dining areas were an important feature. Stone or concrete tables were often incorporated into the design, surrounded on three sides by wide benches with loose cushions, on which guests reclined to eat and drink. These dining areas were sometimes situated beneath arbours or pergolas, with uprights of timber, brick, stone or marble. Timber crosspieces formed open roofs and, when covered in vines or ornamental climbers, created dappled shade under which guests could dine in comfort.

All gardens – large or small, urban or rural – had a supply of water in the form of small canals, pools, dipping tanks and the like. Lucius Junius Moderatus Columella wrote a series of books on farming in the 1st century AD, which also touched on horticulture, and he advised that a garden should be made close to a natural water supply such as a stream or river. In the hot Mediterranean climate water was essential, not only for

A garden in Pompeii with a canal and nymphaeum

Opposite, top: **This view through the atrium of the House of the Vettii in Pompeii shows the** impluvium, *used to collect water, and the peristyle garden beyond.*

Opposite, bottom: **The** impluvium *at the House of the Faun in Pompeii was decorated with a bronze statue of a dancing faun*

Architecture in the Roman garden

Three important architectural features were common to both urban gardens and the formal garden spaces that adjoined larger rural villas:

- A colonnade was a row of evenly spaced columns.

- A portico was a roofed colonnade that was attached to a building. It could run around a central courtyard or the building's exterior, providing a sheltered and shaded place from which to admire the garden or the wider landscape and the view beyond.

- A peristyle was a large open courtyard surrounded by a portico within the centre of a Roman house.

The columns that formed such a crucial part of the Roman garden were often carved from stone; however, they also might be constructed from brick and then coated in plaster to give the appearance of stone. During the Roman period it was popular to copy Greek column designs and

these were later described by Leon Battista Alberti, a 15th-century Renaissance architect:

- Doric – ... *Some artists therefore among the Dorians ... were the first to endeavour to improve [the column] by making it round, so as to look like a cup covered with a square tile; and because it seemed somewhat too squat, they raised it higher by lengthening the neck ...*

- Ionic – ... *[Some] did not like to see it so naked, nor with so long a neck, and therefore added to it the imitation of the bark of a tree hanging down on each side, which by its convolution inwards, or volute, embraced the sides of the cup ...*

- Corinthian – ... *Next came the Corinthians ... [who] disliking the squat cup, made use of a high vase covered with leaves, in imitation of one seen on the tomb of a young maiden ...*

De Re Aedificatoria (The Ten Books of Architecture), 1485

watering plants and maintaining fish pools, but for aesthetic and sensory pleasure. It was valued as a still and reflective surface in large pools and for its movement and noise in fountains or moving watercourses. As engineering and technological skills became more refined, it became easier to transport water into gardens and practical watercourses were often made into ornamental rills or canals. In urban areas water was brought via aqueducts and pipes into towns for public use. In contrast, owners of rural villas had to look for natural water sources that they could tap into or divert for irrigation purposes.

An ornamental pool at the House of Meleager in Pompeii

Opposite, left: **The peristyle from the 1st century AD Villa of Poppaea at Oplontis**

Opposite, right: **Detail of an engraving showing Doric, Ionic and Corinthian columns**

Plants, though important to Romans, were often used in a stylish, almost minimalist way. Mass plantings or hedges of box, rosemary and even acanthus seem to have been popular and fruit trees like pomegranates, olives and citrus were grown in pots. Mixed borders with shrubs, herbs and flowering plants were sometimes created, though they seem to have been less common than simple, orderly planting. Avenues of trees and trained climbers were planted and it was the Romans who perfected the art of manipulating plants into elaborate and decorative shapes, which we now call topiary, after the Latin *topiarius* meaning 'ornamental gardener'. In addition a range of different grafting techniques, propagation methods and cultivation skills were practised during the Roman period. Cato the Elder wrote *De Agri Cultura* around 160 BC and, though much of his advice relates to agriculture rather than horticulture, it shows a sophisticated knowledge of propagation and cultivation techniques that would also have applied to ornamental gardening.

It is clear from archaeological excavations that the Romans also understood about the importance of improving soil for plant cultivation, as studies of soil samples show that animal or human manure was sometimes added. Columella's text on farming, written as poetry, is a particularly valuable source of information about garden practice in Roman times. While some of his advice could happily be applied to 21st-century

A detail from the painting on the wall of the garden at the House of the Marine Venus in Pompeii

gardening, such as the successive sowing of annual vegetables, sacrificing a dog to the goddess Rubigo to cure mildew might not be so popular today.

Urban gardens

A great deal of information about Roman town gardens is provided by excavations in Pompeii, the town where life was effectively frozen in time following the eruption of Vesuvius in AD 79. Volcanic ash covered and preserved buildings and their inhabitants for almost 1,700 years and archaeological investigation has provided us with a macabre but detailed snapshot of every day life in a bustling Roman port. In addition to other valuable information, archaeologists began unearthing Pompeian gardens in the early 20th century, revealing what urban, domestic plots looked like and how they were used.

As well as generally following the pattern of an open courtyard with a surrounding portico, distinct areas were often dedicated to vegetable plots to provide the household with fresh food. Ornate features included pools, fountains, mosaics, statues, ornaments, and stone or marble furniture. Some Roman houses had paintings of gardens on the boundary walls of their open courtyards to give the illusion of a view beyond the enclosed space; garden murals were also painted on interior walls to give illusory views, like the indoor garden paintings of the House of the Golden Bracelet, which depict an idealised vision of a garden filled with a variety of plants and trees as well as birds, garden statuary and water features.

A painting of an idealised garden from the House of the Golden Bracelet in Pompeii

Archaeologists have unearthed not only the layout of the buildings and gardens or courtyards in Pompeii, but have also been able to identify where and how plants were grown and can often name specific species. The remains of large pots that once held soil show that plants were grown in containers and Roman writers discuss growing young trees in clay pots – the

pot could then be broken before planting the tree in the ground so that its roots could continue to grow. Plant pots have been found in pits during the excavation of Roman gardens, including those in Pompeii where many pots had holes pierced in the bottom and lower body to allow roots to reach out into the soil. Other evidence for planting techniques includes scarring on walls where fruit trees or wall shrubs were tied and formally trained, while planting holes next to the remnants of columns or upright pillars show how pergolas and arbours were decorated with climbing plants. Due to the unique situation of Pompeii's destruction, archaeologists have also been able to make plaster or cement casts of the cavities left by roots and even tree trunks – a technique first used to make casts of bodies buried under the volcanic debris. These casts have been studied by botanists, giving us an insight into the types of plants and trees grown in Pompeian gardens.

Wealthier Romans often lived just outside the town in the suburbs, where there was more space for bigger houses and gardens and the journey into nearby towns like Pompeii was relatively quick and easy. The gardens might have been up to an acre in size, with the character of a walled garden, though the architectural features of colonnades, peristyles and atria were still integral to the villa. In large gardens it was also common to have an area set aside as an orchard.

Cement cast of a tree buried during the destruction of Pompeii

Opposite: **Common rue,** Ruta graveolens

Pompeian gardens

The House of the Vettii (c AD 50) clearly illustrates the style of house and garden wealthy Pompeians would have enjoyed. It was owned by two rich brothers who were identified by inscribed rings found on the site. The courtyard garden today is virtually an exact replica of the original, possible because the preserving ash from the eruption of Vesuvius fell and settled so quickly that details as small as the imprints of individual flowers could be detected.

The interior and protected exterior walls beneath the colonnade are decorated with elaborate murals and the central peristyle garden, open to the sky, was predominantly paved, with symmetrical, rectangular beds running down either side. A large number of ornaments were placed around the garden, including marble basins and bronze and marble statues on pillars, and the fluted stone columns that support the colonnade are decorated to look like marble. Rainwater was collected in the atrium, then diverted to the garden through lead pipes for irrigation and to feed the pools. The House of the Vettii clearly demonstrates the close relationship between the interior and exterior of a Roman town house.

Other Pompeiian houses show some of the classic features of Roman urban gardens: the atrium at the House of the Silver Wedding beneath which a pool was located to collect rainwater for house and garden use, murals and frescos depicting garden scenes at the House of the Marine Venus, a fountain at the House of the Small Fountain and an elaborate pool and canal system at the House of Octavius Quartio.

Garden ornaments and furniture have also been unearthed, including sundials and plaques. The latter were called *pinax* if wall mounted and *oscillum* when carved on both sides and hung from a chain. Elaborately carved stone or marble tables and seats have also been found, though in parts of the garden that were designed to be outdoor dining rooms, furniture was of a more static, permanent nature. Built-in couches surrounded a central table and these would have had removable cushions so that the Romans could eat comfortably in their preferred reclining position.

Such archaeological evidence demonstrates how the urban Roman garden was a highly sociable place, designed for eating, talking and relaxing.

One of the ornamental pools from the House of Octavius Quartio

The peristyle garden at the House of Menander

Opposite, left: **Bronze statues in the peristyle at the House of the Vettii**

Opposite, right: **A photomechanical print c 1890–1900 showing the peristyle at the House of the Vettii**

Villa gardens

Further from the town, in rural and coastal areas, large villas were built either as first or second homes, with the owner spending much of his or her life in a townhouse, retreating to the country for summer breaks and to deal with farming business. Villas on the coast were usually built purely for pleasure and relaxation, but those in the country were often at the centre of a working agricultural estate. The outdoor spaces directly adjoining these larger villas followed a similar layout to that of small urban courtyards, but additional land allowed the owners to expand their horticultural activities, both spatially and creatively.

These larger sites were often designed as a series of individual formal spaces, divided by hedges, walls, columns, statuary and arbours. Each was linked to an adjoining area by the use of formal design devices such as axes and focal points. This technique created a series of individual gardens that none the less related to one another, producing a sense of unity throughout the larger garden. In this we see the origins of the idea of the 'garden room' – a concept often attributed to 20th-century garden design.

Another Roman garden design concept used in rural or coastal sites was to be adopted and adapted in 18th-century British gardens: that of 'borrowing' the view of the wider landscape beyond the garden boundaries. Views were often framed or emphasised using avenues of trees or structural features such as arches and colonnades. For example, at the imperial villa of Livia at Prima Porta (outside Rome), an ornamental garden in a small peristyle was juxtaposed with the view of the natural beauty of the mountains that lay beyond. In general, the relationship between house and landscape was to become increasingly important to garden design philosophy in the centuries to follow, but it is clear that the Romans were already experimenting with such ideas.

Similarly, one of the motivations of 18th-century landscape design was to show man's dominance of and power over nature. This was done in a variety of ways. Rivers were realigned and hills and valleys re-contoured in an effort to create 'perfect landscapes', but yet again the Romans had done it first. It was they who first ordered sloping hillsides into regular terraces suitable for grape production (at the same time being the forerunners of the 18th-century *ferme ornée* movement where practical and aesthetic landscape considerations were combined). Furthermore, in town and country alike, Romans were already experts in diverting and managing the flow of water along aqueducts and canals.

Evidence from Pliny the Younger

The letters of Pliny the Younger (AD 61–113) provide valuable information about Roman gardens, in particular those, like his own, that surrounded large country villas. He had one home at Laurentium, which was to the south of Rome near the sea, and from here he travelled to town with relative ease. It was clearly somewhere he loved.

An engraving by George Cooke of Pliny the Younger

> … *my Laurentine place is such a joy to me … It is seventeen miles from Rome so that it is possible to spend the night there after necessary business is done … there are two colonnades, rounded like the letter 'D', which enclose a small but pleasant courtyard. This makes a splendid retreat in bad weather, being protected by windows and even more by an overhanging roof*

… [The dining room] has folding doors or windows as large as the doors all round, so that at the front and sides it seems to look out onto three seas, and at the back it has a view through the inner hall, the courtyard with the two colonnades, and the entrance hall to the woods and mountains in the distance.

Letter to Gallus

He continues with a description of the garden at this villa:

A model based on Pliny the Younger's description of his seaside villa at Laurentium near Rome

… [The dining room] looks out upon the garden … The gestatio [an area for exercise] is bordered round with box, and where that is decayed, with rosemary, for the box, wherever sheltered by the buildings, grows plentifully, but where it lies open and exposed to the weather and spray from the sea, though at some distance from it, it withers up. Next to the gestatio is a shady vine plantation, the path of which is so soft and easy to tread you may walk bare foot upon it. The garden is chiefly planted with fig and mulberry trees, to which this soil is favourable …

Letter to Gallus

Pliny's second villa in Tuscany was his country home. It was
part of a working estate and it is clear from his
correspondence that Pliny was a knowledgeable farmer,
though like many successful Roman businessmen, an absentee
landlord for much of the time, returning for short breaks and
to attend to business matters.

> *Other people visit their estates to come away*
> *richer than before, but I go only to return the*
> *poorer. I had sold my grape harvest to the*
> *dealers, who were eager to buy, when the price*
> *quoted at the time was tempting and the*
> *prospects seemed good …*

Letter to Calvisius Rufus

Pliny's Tuscan garden, which lay at the foot of the mountains,
experienced a harsher winter climate than the one at
Laurentium and he refers to cold and frosty weather,
necessitating the planting of laurel to replace myrtles and
olives; similar substitutes were also necessary in Romano-
British gardens. He speaks of the garden being set in a natural
amphitheatre, surrounded by mountains and woods, with
vineyards on the lower slopes and meadows and cornfields on
the flat plain below. His house stood on the lower slope of the
hill, facing south with a sunny colonnade.

In front of the colonnade is a terrace laid out
with box hedges clipped into different shapes,
from which a bank slopes down, also with
animals cut out of box facing each other on
either side. On the level below there waves – or
I might have said ripples – a bed of acanthus.
All round the path is hedged by bushes which
are trained and cut into different shapes, and
then a drive, oval like a racecourse, inside which
are various box figures and clipped dwarf shrubs.
The whole garden is enclosed by a dry stone
wall which is hidden from sight by a box hedge
planted in tiers; outside is a meadow, as well
worth seeing for its natural beauty as the formal
garden I have described ...

Letter to Domitius Apollinaris

When the Emperor Hadrian built his villa and garden near Tivoli outside Rome in AD 118–34, he created an extravagant three-dimensional reminder of the many provinces in the Roman Empire that he had visited and admired, especially Greece and Egypt, whose architecture and luxurious style particularly inspired him. Hadrian, together with other rich and powerful Romans, set a trend that was to be mimicked throughout Europe over the following centuries: creating large and extravagant gardens that demonstrated their wealth and influence.

The excavation of the Villa Adriana was one of the most important archaeological explorations of the Renaissance and the site was studied by the likes of Michaelangelo, Palladio and Leonardo da Vinci. The original excavation was overseen by architect Pirro Ligorio, who was building the remarkable Villa d'Este nearby. His motives were probably questionable, however, as not only ideas but also artifacts, including statues and marble, were taken from the Roman site to decorate the new villa and garden. Such pilfering continued over the centuries and, when young British gentlemen visited as part of the 18th-century Grand Tour,

it was common practice to take souvenirs from the site. Indeed, the Exedra – designed for Lord Burlington by William Kent in the 1730s – originally incorporated three statues supposedly from Hadrian's Villa. However, whilst many of the expensive materials that decorated the walls and floors of Hadrian's villa and garden have been lost, a great deal remains to demonstrate the luxurious lifestyle of this Roman emperor.

Hillside slopes were excavated on an extensive scale over 150 acres to provide materials and a workable landscape for the villa, associated buildings, roads and the surrounding gardens. Roman engineers used gravity to power the many fountains and water features that decorated the lower gardens. The result was an architectural mammoth, a garden on a scale so grand it could even accommodate recreations of the Emperor's favourite Greek valley, the Vale of Tempe found to the north of the villa, and the Canopus canal in Alexandria. The latter was surrounded by stone statuary, including columns carved as figures that were copies of the original caryatids from the Acropolis in Athens. Beautifully proportioned lintels topped the columns, alternately flat and

arched, and stone representations of the gods were placed between the columns. The stone architecture was perfectly reflected in the still water of the canal.

Another striking water garden, the Maritime Garden, was developed by the emperor within a high, circular stone wall and had at its centre an island surrounded by a wide moat. Moving bridges allowed people to claim privacy once on the island by rotating the structures so they faced into the water, thus preventing access by others. Stone columns enclosed the circular walk that surrounded the moat, creating large 'windows' through which the island could be viewed.

Top: A reconstruction drawing of Hadrian's Villa by F Buhlmann

Bottom: The Canopus Canal at Hadrian's Villa

Opposite: A view of the Exedra at Chiswick House where copies of the original statues taken from Hadrian's Villa are displayed

create a small formal Roman garden

The two basic rules you need to bear in mind when thinking about designing a formal, Roman-style garden are simplicity and symmetry. Don't over-decorate or over-plant the garden, and if possible work on level ground; where there are changes in level create steps and terraces rather than slopes. The beauty of this style of garden is that it is low maintenance and looks good all year round.

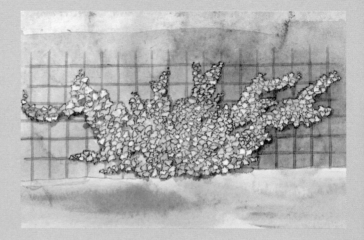

The basic 'ingredients' and instructions given below will enable you to create the character and feel of a small Roman garden, though the proportions and details will need to be adapted for each individual site. The design outlined here is for a space measuring 5 x 10m. It incorporates the following elements:

- ❖ Trained ivy boundaries

- ❖ Box hedging

- ❖ Plant pots and plants

- ❖ A water feature

- ❖ Bay 'lollipop' topiary

- ❖ An area of mosaic (see pp 54–5)

- ❖ A vine-covered structure (see pp 68–9)

Boundaries

It would be very expensive and require specialist skills to build a stone or brick wall around the garden. Instead, think about making 'green walls' using ivy. Ivy is a self-clinging plant but needs a structure to cling to if it is to climb and the simplest way to make one is to attach a heavy-duty square trellis to wooden or concrete fence posts fixed firmly into the ground. If your site is surrounded by panel fencing it is always a good idea to fix a trellis to the front of this as ivy can cause a great deal of damage to timber fences; this way the trellis will take the brunt of the

Box hedging

Use common box, *Buxus sempervirens*, rather than the dwarf form 'Suffruticosa', as you need deep, strong hedges for best effect. Plant young shrubs around 8in (200mm) apart in well-prepared ground that has been dug over and enriched with organic matter and a slow-release fertiliser. During the early years while the hedge is still developing it should be cut in late spring after growth has slowed down, removing about a third of the new wood. Though this seems like 'two steps forward and one back' it will help you to develop a thick hedge. Once the hedge is the height and width you require (and you need it to be approximately 1½ft (0.5m) tall and wide), trim it back to the same level each year.

Containers and pots for the plants

Various types of containers can be used in your garden, such as large, plain terracotta pots or ones made from reconstituted stone. Use broken pots, large sharp stones or even lumps of polystyrene in the bottom to aid drainage. Fill up the container with multipurpose or soil-based compost, adding a handful of slow-release fertiliser granules in the top layer. All the containers should be planted identically in your

growth. Use small blocks of wood to secure the trellis approximately 2in (50mm) away from the fence.

Young ivy plants in small pots will grow quickly and, though the young growth might need a little help initially to cling onto the trellis, it will not be long before they cling on their own. In the early years try and encourage the growth upwards and sideways to cover the boundary in a flat fan shape – don't let it bunch up. Eventually you will need to clip over the ivy each year with shears to keep the growth flat to the boundary.

create a small formal Roman garden

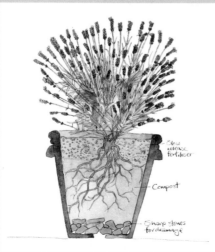

formal garden. On a sunny site use 3–5 young herbs, such as lavender, hyssop, rosemary or rue, which will fill out the container in a year; on a more shaded site you could use large box balls, ivy or holly. Bear's breeches, *Acanthus mollis*, would also look good in pots though it might need to be watered daily and kept out of bright sunlight. In late spring each year add a handful more of the fertiliser granules to the compost.

Water feature

Roman gardens usually had some form of pool or fountain and if you have the space and funds you could include one in your garden, though for more ambitious designs you may have to commission a professional to build it for you. Choose a formal shape for the pool, ideally square or rectangular, and position it at a focal point – perhaps at the end of a path or vista or at the

meeting point of four paths. The inside of the pool should either be left as a concrete finish with a special sealant applied to the surface or it can be finished in mosaic tiles.

Bay laurel 'lollipops'

It takes several years to train a bay laurel cutting into a lollipop shape, so you may wish to purchase 'ready made' specimens. These can be quite expensive but if you buy quite young plants with a slender trunk and small head, it is far more economical and they grow relatively quickly from this stage. The plants have a tendency to sucker from the base, so look out for young shoots emerging from the soil and gently peel these away from the root before they become too established. In containers, use a John Innes Number 3 type soil-based compost, and add an additional handful of granular feed into the top few centimetres of soil at the start of each growing season. You may need to clip the heads using secateurs a couple of times each year to keep them tidy, but in the first few years you need to find a balance between removing long straggly growth and letting the head develop and expand. Aim at removing one-third of new growth each time you cut until the head reaches the size you are happy with, then simply clip to maintain this framework each time.

Gardens in the Mediterranean region were designed to cope with hot dry weather and certain adaptations must have been made when translating them to the British climate, particularly in respect of plants. Agricola, Governor of Britain in the 1st century AD, told his son-in-law Tacitus that 'the climate is wretched with its frequent rains and mists...' but he noted that the soil was good. Though wetter than the Mediterranean, Britain's climate was relatively mild during the Roman period, so many imported plants would have survived and more tender specimens such as olive and citrus trees could possibly have been grown in pots placed in protected areas within the garden.

Though most of the information about Roman gardens comes from Italian remains and literary and artistic references, there is some evidence of these early gardens in Britain, the most extensive being at Fishbourne in West Sussex. Due to its scale and grandeur, Fishbourne is not thought to be typical of Roman architecture or garden-making in Britain; nevertheless it demonstrates how Roman ideas and styles were imported into and adapted in this newly conquered land.

A chance discovery of a Roman settlement at Fishbourne in the 1960s led to an archaeological dig that unearthed the remains of a royal palace and garden dating back to AD 75. It is believed to have been the residence of Cogidubnus, a native

Formal pools, box hedging, topiary and colonnaded architecture were popular in Roman gardens and remain so today

'king and legate to the emperor in Britain'. The site is one of the most important sources of information about Roman gardens in Britain, as it reveals the layout and design of that original garden. During excavations, original beds and planting holes were identified from the soil that was brought in to enhance the existing acidic gravel and improve upon what was effectively builders' rubble, originally used to level the site. The scale of garden-making and maintenance at Fishbourne must have demanded a large workforce, which would have included skilled craftsmen and gardeners as well as labourers, perhaps all brought here from Italy.

The main garden was enclosed on all sides by the wings of the building and was dissected by a wide central path running from the entrance hall at one side to the audience chamber at the other. The central path was flanked by alternating rectangular and curved bedding trenches, and narrower paths – also flanked by a variety of planting beds – ran around the boundary of the garden. Analysis of the soil indicates that hedges surrounded all these paths. Common box, *Buxus sempervirens*, was a popular Roman hedge plant and was known to grow well in Britain, so it is assumed that the hedges at Fishbourne were planted with box, though no actual evidence exists. Sections of the present garden have been replanted with large box hedges today and rows of espaliered apple trees now also line some of the paths. These have been

The excavated bedding trenches beside the central pathway in the courtyard garden at Fishbourne

Opposite: **Aerial photograph of Fishbourne showing the outline of one wing of the villa and part of the reconstructed courtyard garden**

planted to follow the excavated remains of planting holes alternating with wooden post-holes, which suggest trained trees of some kind were originally used. Pliny the Younger recommended training fruit trees in this way, suggesting that they would bring a rustic air to a formal garden. Due to the

Box hedging has been planted in the original bedding trenches at Fishbourne

scarcity of pollen samples and plant remains at Fishbourne, botanical evidence from other Romano-British sites, along with classical literary and artistic sources, have provided information for the reconstruction and it is assumed that popular Roman plants such as acanthus, lilies, roses and woody herbs like rosemary would have been grown there.

The exact position of the paths, columns and courtyard within the main garden became clear during excavation work, as well as evidence of elaborate fountains, for which the feeding pipework has been unearthed. Fragments of marble have led archaeologists to think that pools or basins were positioned within the recesses of the box hedge in the garden.

A planter pot from Fishbourne with a drainage hole in the base and ventilation holes in the sides

Other gardens at Fishbourne included a possible kitchen garden to supply the palace, where a variety of fruits, herbs and vegetables would have been cultivated. It is likely that figs, wild strawberries, beans, lentils, cabbages, carrots, fennel and dill were amongst the edible plants grown there. It is also possible that enclosed peristyle gardens were located in the north and east wings of the building. Moving away from the palace to the south, the gardens seem to have become less formal, with trees and shrubs planted more randomly, perhaps in an attempt to integrate the gardens with the wider natural landscape.

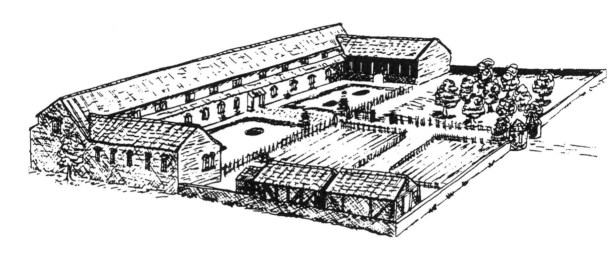

While Fishbourne is the most well-known Roman garden in Britain, other information sourced from a variety of different Romano-British sites provides clues for archaeologists and garden historians who have been able to develop firm ideas of what gardens looked like and how they were cultivated throughout the years of Roman occupation in Britain. At Frocester Court in Gloucestershire, improved earth in the original planting areas suggests that compost was made on site and used to improve soil in the growing beds. The villa at Latimer in Buckinghamshire has evidence of formal planting styles in more utilitarian or productive gardens, with rows of vegetables or fruit trees laid out, and Chedworth Roman Villa in Gloucestershire is thought to have had a large lawned courtyard. The technique of growing young plants in terracotta pots, then transplanting these, pot and all into the ground, must have been used at Eccles, Kent, as fragments of broken pots have been found in planting holes on that site.

The 350 years of Roman occupation was a relatively settled time and it is only in times of peace and stability that ornamental gardening can be practised in any society. In the 5th century AD, as their empire began to collapse, the Romans withdrew from Britain and the country entered a poorly documented period known as the Dark Ages. It was not until the medieval period, several centuries later, that life once again became sufficiently peaceful for ornamental gardening to continue to develop and small, formally laid out gardens once again began to appear.

Aerial photograph of Chedworth Roman Villa in 1962 showing the lawned courtyard

create a Roman-inspired mosaic

Detailed Roman mosaics were works of art created by skilled craftspeople and even today artists spend many hours designing and making equally intricate work. Nevertheless, there are ways for those with less experience to create the character of a Roman mosaic, either traditional in style or with a contemporary twist.

Roman mosaics were made from a variety of materials including tiles (or *tesserae*), pebbles, marble and terracotta. The most popular materials were the small square tiles laid individually to create a detailed picture or pattern. The range of building and decorating supplies available to us today provide a wealth of material suitable for mosaic work and sheets of small tiles fixed to a net base, available in many DIY outlets, are ideal for this project. Just make sure you use tiles and cement adhesive that are suitable for outdoor use.

The following instructions are for a small, simple black and white design that can be laid in one session. The pattern and style are very simple, so the mosaic should be relatively easy to lay. If you feel more confident or have experience you might want to try a more intricate design, use more colours or work on a larger scale.

The floor mosaic must be laid on a clean, firm and level concrete base that has a slight fall to ensure water drains from the surface. The fall should be approximately ½in per foot (10mm per 300mm).

❖ Using a notched trowel, spread a ¼in (5mm) layer of exterior-quality tile mortar across the concrete.

❖ Set up some string guides to help you position the mosaic and to keep the lines within the design square and parallel.

❖ Cut the central pattern of 45 small black tiles from the larger net-based tile.

❖ Using the string lines as a guide, lay this pattern in the centre of the design.

❖ Now cut out the next layer of the design of 76 white tiles from the large net-based tile. This should fit tightly round the black central pattern.

The remaining layers will have to be cut from sections of the larger tiles, but the pieces will join together to make the surrounding borders. You can add to these as many times as you wish to make the size of mosaic you require for your area of concrete, simply alternating black and white layers.

Leave the mortar to set, loosely covering the mosaic with a plastic sheet.

When the mortar is dry clean all the tiles, making sure any residue of mortar is removed.

Use a rubber float to apply the grout, holding it at a 45 degree angle and working the paste into all the joints. Another clean rubber float can be used to remove excess grout from the tiles while still wet.

After 15 minutes, use a damp sponge to wipe over the surface of the tiles, being careful not to damage the lines of grout.

Cover with a plastic sheet and leave to dry for 24 hours.

Plants

The Greek philosopher and naturalist Theophrastus (372–288 BC) made an early foray into plant classification in his *Enquiry into Plants* around 300 BC and there followed an increasing interest in and recording of the uses of plants. The most well-known Roman treatise on plants was found in Pliny the Elder's (AD 23–79) *Historia Naturalis*. This work, made up of 37 volumes, was effectively an early exploration of nature and science, and considered such subjects as astronomy, geography, zoology and botany, as well as art and architecture. It is the sections on botany that hold the most detailed information for garden historians, with chapters on trees, olives and other fruiting trees, flowers and herbs, wild and medicinal plants, along with information about their cultivation:

15th-century illuminated letter from Pliny the Elder's Historia Naturalis *showing a man hewing trees*

> *Invariably when mistletoe is sown it does not
> grow unless it has passed through bird droppings
> – especially pigeons' and thrushes'. Such is its
> nature that it will not sprout unless matured in
> the stomach of a bird. Its maximum height is
> 18 inches and it is always green and bushy.
> The male mistletoe is fertile, the female barren,
> except that even a fertile plant sometimes does
> not bear berries.*

Historia Naturalis, Book XVI: Forest Trees

Opposite: **Common medlar,** Mespilus germanica

Another important source was *De Materia Medica*, a significant medical herbal written by the Greek physician Dioscorides, who travelled with the Roman armies in the 1st century AD. In this book, Dioscorides described how to grow, harvest, store and use many different plants for medical purposes. The Romans used plants for a variety of remedies. Fennel calmed the nerves, garlic was used as a daily health supplement and henbane as a painkiller. Rosemary, sage and fennel were all used for their healing properties and over 40 potions were made from mustard. Such medical knowledge would have been brought to Britain when the Romans invaded and added to the existing remedies and cures already practised by the natives. Indeed, an accounts record on a writing tablet from the Roman fort at Vindolanda in Northumberland, which might have been an inventory of medical supplies or the ingredients of a medical recipe, lists various plant products, including anise, berries, beans and mustard seed. We still use many plants to cure the same ailments to which they were applied by the Romans, though today these are usually produced commercially, with the plants or synthetic substitutes forming a base to more sophisticated mixtures: fig juice as a laxative, cucumbers to soothe eyes, mint to ease stomach upset and opium poppy for pain relief and sleep inducement.

An illustration of common vervain, Verbena officinalis, *from an 11th-century manuscript of Dioscorides' herbal*

Plants and flowers were also used in religious ceremonies and many people believed they had magical associations. Vervain, *Verbena officinalis*, decorated temples and altars and was carried by soldiers for protection. It was also used in love potions as vervain was associated with Venus, the goddess of love. The Roman version of our pagan-based May Day celebrations was the two-week festival of 'Floralia', which celebrated Flora, the goddess of flowers, during which buildings were bedecked with freshly cut plants and flowers. The long, trailing stems of the lesser periwinkle, *Vinca minor*, formed the base of wreaths and garlands, with larger flowers such as roses woven through the stems. Then as now, myrtle, *Myrtus communis*, was used in bridal wreaths and bay laurel, *Laurus nobilis*, a favourite decorative plant, was worn as a head wreath by emperors at victory celebrations. Laurel was also used in worship of the gods Apollo and Jupiter and in many other aspects of life, as a culinary, medicinal, decorative and symbolic plant.

As well as being appreciated for important practical uses, plants were also enjoyed simply for their beauty. As the Romans' interest in ornamental gardening became more sophisticated their appreciation of decorative plants grew. Gardens in the hot sunny climates of southern Europe and North Africa relied on drought-tolerant herbs and sun-loving plants such as olives, citrus and oleander. Also vital to enjoying

A panel from the Ara Pacis in Rome depicting a procession of members of the imperial family, some of whom are wearing laurel crowns, with geometric and floral motifs decorating the lower bands of the altar

A 3rd-century AD mosaic from St Romain-en-Gal in France depicting labourers harvesting olives

the garden was the provision of shade, either from vine-clad arbours and pergolas or from the canopy of cypress and plane trees. Evidence of these plantings comes from archaeological excavations and illustrations on mosaics and other Roman art objects, as well as from the writing and poetry of the period.

> ... perhaps I too would be singing how careful
> cultivation ornaments rich gardens,
> and of the twice-flowering rose-beds of Paestum,
> how the endive delights in the streams it drinks,

and the green banks in parsley,

and how the gourd, twisting over the ground,

swells its belly:

nor would I be silent about the late-flowering

narcissi, or the curling stem of acanthus,

the pale ivy, and the myrtle that loves the shore.

The Georgics, Virgil, c 29 BC

While flowers were enjoyed and appreciated, most Roman gardens were architectural in style, relying on structure in the form of trained and clipped evergreen plants such as myrtle, box, yew and cypress and even ivy which was used as a green wall or backdrop.

… I praised your landscape gardener: he has so covered everything with ivy, both the foundation-wall of the villa and the spaces between the columns of the walk, that, upon my word, those Greek statues seemed to be engaging in fancy gardening, and to be showing off the ivy …

Letter from Cicero (106–43 BC) to his brother Quintus

Though it was to be another 1,000 years after the Roman invasion of Britain before dedicated plant hunting was to become a fashionable pursuit, it is clear that these sophisticated people already had an appreciation of plants for their aesthetic qualities, as well as for medicinal, aromatic, religious and culinary uses. Many Roman authors record that there was demand for certain exotic plants such as silphium, seemingly a form of 'giant fennel' that was commonly used as a rich seasoning in cooking or for medicinal purposes. Silphium was obtained from Cyrene in Libya and was so important to the economy of this area that it was represented on their coins. By the 1st century AD it was believed to be extinct due to high demand.

A silver coin from Cyrene with an image of the silphium plant on its reverse

Plants in Roman Britain

There does not seem to have been an international exchange of plants purely for ornamental purposes during the Roman period, but the ongoing movement of people and goods across Europe and North Africa meant that for the first time plants were continually crossing boundaries. Pliny the Elder records in *Historia Naturalis* how plants and trees were imported to Italy from the Eastern Mediterranean and the Near East, and explains how these were then transported throughout the empire. In Book 15, Chapter 30 he records how L Lucullus brought the cherry tree to Italy in 74 BC, writing 'He was the first to introduce this tree from Pontus, and now, in the course of one hundred and twenty years, it has travelled beyond the Ocean, and arrived in Britannia even.' The transportation of plants throughout the Empire must have been a demanding practice. It is clear that plants were grown commercially in terracotta pots in which they were transported and often planted.

A wide variety of plants were grown and as many as possible were brought to Britain in an attempt to cultivate them in this colder, wetter climate. Citrus trees and possibly olives were grown in containers that were probably taken into sheltered areas for winter and, as we have already seen from the writing of Pliny the Younger, hardier specimens could be substituted for tender plants out in the main garden. Some of the introduced plants were so well suited to their new surroundings that they were cultivated from then on and effectively became adopted as a native plant in the recipient country. Common box, *Buxus sempervirens*, is a native species that was brought into cultivation by the Romans and it is now considered a quintessentially English garden plant.

It is not always clear from the pollen and plant remains identified by archaeologists if specific plants were actually grown in Britain, or whether flowers, seeds, vegetables or fruits were imported. However, there are some specific findings that make it clear that certain plants were growing in the ground: for example box clippings have been found at

Winterton villa in Lincolnshire, cabbage roots at Chesterholm fort on Hadrian's Wall and significant amounts of pollen from the common mallow found in the waste deposits at Bearsden near Glasgow. The charred remains of asparagus, columbine and beet – interpreted as the possible burning of garden waste – have been found at the Roman town of Alcester in Warwickshire. There is also evidence for a substantial vineyard at Wollaston in Northamptonshire, demonstrating that grapes were cultivated in this northern extreme of the empire; indeed later medieval vineyards make it evident that vines could be grown on quite a large scale in Britain. In addition, we can assume that certain plants must have been cultivated in Roman Britain, for example the fact that mulberry fruits are difficult to transport, so evidence of their remains in London, Silchester and York suggests trees must have been grown nearby. There is also evidence in Britain of the ritual use of plants. Box leaves in a late Roman burial site have been interpreted as a possible symbol of everlasting life due to their evergreen nature, while bay leaves that were found beneath the head of a wealthy female buried in London are thought to have been used as some sort of pillow or possibly even a funerary wreath. Plants were also placed on funeral pyres: a Roman pyre site in a London cemetery included the burned remains of lentils, peas, beans and one solitary grape pip.

An illustration of common mallow, **Malva sylvestris,** *from an 11th-century manuscript of Dioscorides' herbal*

Opposite: **Black mulberry, Morus nigra**

The grape and the vine

Probably the most important Roman plant was the vine, which was grown in large vineyards and provided grapes for the wine that was drunk in diluted form by Roman citizens every day. Much of the Roman literary evidence about the cultivation of plants focuses on vines, with Columella, Cato the Elder, both Plinys – Elder and Younger – and others instructing on the propagation, cultivation and harvesting of grapes. Pliny the Elder talked about the history of the vine and writes of ancient trunks that were used as columns and pillars. He claims that vinewood has the longest life of any timber and mentions a staircase in Cyprus that was carved from a single vine.

As well as providing grapes, vines were valuable as garden plants and Pliny the Elder thought the perfume of vine flowers was unequalled by any other, which would have added to its value in the garden. In addition, the structural quality of vines, trained up posts and along overhead supports similar to pergolas and arbours would have been valued. Their foliage provided dappled shade from the sun while the fruits hung below, for vines grown as garden plants would also have been harvested. Pliny the Elder describes this and other methods of growing and supporting vines:

> … a single vine in the colonnades of the house of Livia at Rome shades the open walks with its trellises and at the same time produces 84 gallons of grape-juice annually …

> … In Campania the vines are tied to poplars; embracing their 'brides' and climbing with unruly arms in a knotted course among their branches, they rise level with their tops, so high up that those hired to harvest the grapes make a point of arranging for a pyre and a grave in the terms of their employment …

> I have even seen whole country houses, as well as other buildings encircled by the shoots and clinging tendrils of a single vine …

Top: *Roman mosaic of a bunch of grapes from Tunisia*

Bottom: *A replanted vineyard and wine vats from a house in Pompeii*

A reconstructed wine press from the Villa of the Mysteries in Pompeii

Vines, when supported by stakes about as tall as a man of medium height, make a shaggy growth and form a whole vineyard from a single cutting.

In some provinces the vine stands by itself without any prop, keeping its limbs close to itself and sustaining a luxuriant growth by virtue of its shortness.

Historia Naturalis, Book XIV: Vines and Viticulture

He concludes his praise of the vine with a stern warning on the effects of drinking too much wine:

… the intoxicated never see the sunrise and so shorten their lives. This is the reason for pale faces, hanging jowls, sore eyes, and trembling hands … The morning after the breath reeks … the memory is dead. This is what people call 'enjoying life'; but while other men daily lose their yesterdays, these people also lose their tomorrows.

Historia Naturalis, Book XIV: Vines and Viticulture

grow and train vines over structures

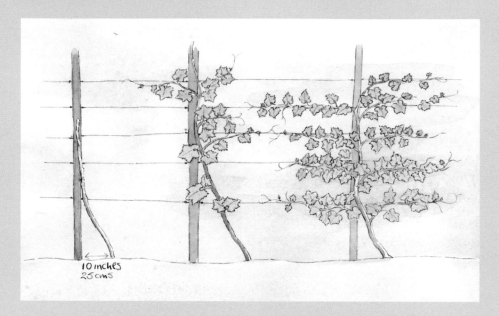

10 inches
25 cms

Unless you live in a very mild part of the country, you may find that grape vines produce little or no edible fruit, but they are nevertheless worth growing for their attractive twining habit and large leaves. Some varieties have foliage that turns red in autumn, such as the hardy 'Brant', which is one of the best for growing outdoors in the UK.

Alternatives to fruiting vines would be the hardy ornamental vines grown for their attractive foliage, such as Japanese crimson glory vine, *Vitis coignetiae*, and Virginia creeper, *Parthenocissus quinquefolia* syn *V quinquefolia,* or alternatively the kiwi fruit vine, *Actinidia deliciosa*, which is unlikely to bear mature fruit in Britain but has wonderful foliage and hairy stems.

You could use either a simple wooden structure or one with brick pillars and timber crosspieces. In either case it must be substantial as over the years the vine will become thick and heavy. If you want the vine to enclose the structure at the sides as well as across the top you will need to fix

strong, galvanised wires horizontally between the uprights, spaced approximately 18in (450mm) apart.

If you want to produce serious crops of grapes from your vine you need to understand the very specific pruning requirements of productive vines and should refer to a specialist manual or encyclopaedia. However, if you are happy to make a decorative feature that will produce some grapes as an added bonus, the following instructions will guide you:

❖ Vines are quite vigorous plants and you will need to allow about 6½ft (2m) between each. They should be planted about 10in (250mm) away from the base of the upright post or pillar, with the top growth leant into the post. This should be tied in place gently but firmly with garden twine attached to a screw eye fixed firmly into the upright.

In the first few growing seasons you need to concentrate on creating a framework for the vine so that it covers the structure both vertically and horizontally without becoming entangled. The important thing to remember about grape vines is that they must always be pruned in winter as they 'bleed' when cut in the growing season.

The new vine should be planted in winter and cut back hard by removing about two-thirds of the upright growth and all the side shoots. You will be left with a rather sorry-looking twig but the new growth that shoots from this in spring will allow you to start to develop a formal framework of wood.

As new growth develops from the top of the vine, begin tying it in gently and vertically through the following growing season without any further pruning – you are aiming to encourage this to grow tall and straight.

As side shoots develop from the upright growth, gently tie these sideways along the wires, nipping out any surplus shoots that you don't need. Continue to tie these gently along the horizontal wires for the rest of the season but pinch back any side shoots from these stems as they develop.

Each year you will need to repeat this process to some extent, cutting back the upright and side stems by two-thirds, though if you are more serious about producing fruiting wood you will find you need to be rather more aggressive. The more vigorous and structured the pruning, the more grapes will be produced.

Over the following years the vine will gradually cover the structure. You need to continue with the winter prune to keep the growth under control and through the growing season nip out any unwanted young shoots as they develop.

The following lists of plants, while not exhaustive, give an indication of plants that were available in Roman Britain. All those plants listed are available in one form or another, whether as seed, container-grown specimens or, in the case of some woodier plants, bare-rooted trees and shrubs. If you want to plant a reproduction Roman garden you might find that some of the plants are not readily available in their simple forms. It is crucial then to decide whether your planting must be authentic or whether it is to be 'in the style of' Roman planting, in which case you will have a wider palette to select from and will find the plants easier to obtain.

Many cultivated forms of plants are only available as container-grown specimens because they are often propagated vegetatively (eg as cuttings or by layering). However, most annuals and many British wildflowers, native or naturalised, are rarely sold in garden centres as established plants because they are short-lived and uneconomical to grow on a commercial scale. Your only option will be to grow them from seed from specialist suppliers.

Please remember that under the Wildlife and Countryside Act it is illegal to uproot any wild plant and to take material from protected species. All the plants listed in this book are available from legitimate sources.

Opium poppy, Papaver somniferum

Plants   Available   Widely available   Seed   Available   Widely available

Unusual   Unusual

BOTANICAL NAME	COMMON NAME	PLANTS	SEED
Flowering / ornamental plants			
Acanthus mollis	Bear's breeches	🌱🌱	◆
Acanthus spinosus	Armed bear's breeches	🌱🌱	◆
Alcea rosea	Hollyhock	🌱	◆
Althaea officinalis	Marsh mallow	🌱	◆ ◆
Aquilegia vulgaris	Common columbine	🌱	◆ ◆
Iris foetidissima	Stinking iris	🌱🌱	◆
Isatis tinctoria	Woad	🌱	◆
Linum usitatissimum	Common flax	🌱	◆
Malva sylvestris	Common mallow	🌱	◆
Narcissus pseudonarcissus	Wild daffodil	🌱	◆
Onopordum acanthium	Cotton thistle	🌱🌱	◆
Papaver somniferum	Opium poppy	🌱	◆
Tanacetum parthenium	Feverfew	🌱	◆
Verbascum thapsus	Great mullein	🌱	◆
Verbena officinalis	Common vervain	🌱	◆
Vinca minor	Lesser periwinkle	🌱	◆
Viola odorata	Sweet violet	🌱🌱	◆
Herbs			
Allium schoenoprasum	Chives	🌱🌱	◆ ◆
Anethum graveolens	Dill	🌱	◆ ◆
Borago officinalis	Borage	🌱	◆ ◆
Carum carvi	Caraway	🌱	◆ ◆
Coriandrum sativum	Coriander	🌱	◆
Levisticum officinale	Lovage	🌱🌱	◆ ◆

BOTANICAL NAME	COMMON NAME	PLANTS	SEED
Mentha spicata	Common mint		
Myrrhis odorata	Sweet cicely		
Origanum vulgare	Oregano		
Nepeta cataria	Catmint		
Petroselinum crispum	Parsley		
Rosmarinus officinalis	Rosemary		
Ruta graveolens	Common rue		
Salvia officinalis	Common sage		
Satureja hortensis	Summer savory		
Satureja montana	Winter savory		
Thymus vulgaris	Common thyme		
Valeriana officinalis	Common valerian		

Trees and Shrubs

Buxus sempervirens	Common box		
Carpinus betulus	Common hornbeam		
Castanea sativa	Sweet chestnut		
Fagus sylvatica	Common beech		
Fraxinus excelsior	Common ash		
Hedera helix	Common ivy		
Ilex aquifolium	Common holly		
Juniperus communis	Common juniper		
Populus alba	White poplar		
Quercus robur	Common oak		
Rosa rubiginosa	Eglantine		
Salix alba	White willow		

BOTANICAL NAME	COMMON NAME	PLANTS	SEED
Sambucus nigra	Common elder	🪴	◆
Taxus baccata	English yew	🪴 🪴	◆

Fruit

Citrus medica	Citron	🪴	◆
Ficus carica	Fig	🪴	◆
Humulus lupulus	Common hop	🪴	◆
Juglans regia	Common walnut	🪴 🪴	◆
Malus sylvestris	Crab apple	🪴	◆
Mespilus germanica	Common medlar	🪴	◆
Morus nigra	Black mulberry	🪴 🪴	◆
Prunus avium	Wild cherry	🪴	◆
Prunus domestica	Plum	Cultivars only	◆
Prunus insititia	Bullace/damson	🪴	◆
Prunus persica	Peach	Cultivars only	◆
Prunus spinosa	Blackthorn	🪴	◆
Pyrus communis	Wild pear	🪴	◆
Rubus fruticosus	Blackberry	🪴	◆
Rubus idaeus	Common raspberry	Cultivars only	◆
Vitis vinifera	Grape vine	🪴	◆

Vegetables

Allium ampeloprasum	Wild leek	🪴	◆ ◆
Allium cepa	Onion	🪴	◆ ◆
Allium sativum	Garlic	🪴	◆
Asparagus officinalis	Common asparagus	🪴	◆
Beta vulgaris	Common beet	🪴	◆ ◆

BOTANICAL NAME	COMMON NAME	PLANTS	SEED
Brassica oleracea	Cabbage	🪴	◆ ◆
Brassica rapa	Turnip	🪴	◆ ◆
Cucumis sativus	Cucumber	🪴	◆ ◆
Lactuca sativa	Lettuce	🪴	◆ ◆
Pisum sativum	Pea	🪴	◆ ◆
Raphanus sativus	Radish	🪴	◆ ◆
Rumex scutatus	French sorrel	🪴	◆ ◆
Smyrnium olusatrum	Alexanders	🪴	◆
Vicia faba	Broad bean	🪴	◆ ◆

Other Roman plants grown in the Mediterranean, possibly Britain

BOTANICAL NAME	COMMON NAME	PLANTS	SEED
Anemone coronaria	Garden anemone	Cultivars only	◆
Arbutus unedo	Strawberry tree	🪴 🪴	◆
Artemisia abrotanum	Southernwood	🪴 🪴	◆
Artemisia absinthium	Wormwood	🪴	◆ ◆
Calendula officinalis	Common marigold	🪴	◆ ◆
Crocus sativus	Saffron	🪴	◆
Erysimum cheiri	Common wallflower	🪴	◆ ◆
Gladiolus communis subsp. *byzantinus*	Byzantine gladiolus	🪴 🪴	◆
Helichrysum italicum	Curry plant	🪴	◆
Helleborus niger	Christmas rose	🪴 🪴	◆
Hyssopus officinalis	Hyssop	🪴 🪴	◆
Laurus nobilis	Bay laurel tree	🪴 🪴	◆
Lavandula angustifolia	Common lavender	🪴 🪴	◆ ◆
Lilium candidum	Madonna lily	🪴	◆
Melissa officinalis	Lemon balm	🪴	◆ ◆

BOTANICAL NAME	COMMON NAME	PLANTS	SEED
Myrtus communis	Common myrtle	🪴🪴	◆
Nerium oleander	Oleander	🪴	◆
Ocimum basilicum	Common basil	🪴	◆ ◆
Olea europaea	Common olive	🪴🪴	◆
Paeonia officinalis	Common peony	🪴	◆
Physalis alkekengi	Chinese lantern	🪴	◆
Pinus pinea	Stone pine	🪴	◆
Prunus armeniaca	Apricot	Cultivars only	◆
Prunus dulcis	Almond	🪴	◆
Punica granatum	Pomegranate	🪴	◆
Saponaria officinalis	Soapwort	🪴	◆
Sempervivum tectorum	Common houseleek	🪴	◆
Tilia platyphyllos	Large-leaved lime	🪴	◆

Scoring system

Unusual = Not listed for sale in the *RHS Plant Finder* or *The Seed Search*

Available = Available from up to 29 listed nurseries

Widely available = Available from over 30 listed nurseries

Common marigold, Calendula officinalis

Further reading

Bowe, Patrick *Gardens of the Roman World*. London: Frances Lincoln, 2004

Campbell-Culver, Maggie *The Origin of Plants: The People and the Plants that have Shaped Britain's Garden History since the Year 1000*. London: Headline, 2001

Carroll, Maureen *Earthly Paradises: Ancient Gardens in History and Archaeology*. London: British Museum Press, 2003

Dark, Petra *The Environment of Britain in the First Millennium AD*. London: Duckworth, 2000

Farrar, Linda *Ancient Roman Gardens*. Stroud: Sutton Publishing, 1998

Healy, John (trans) *Pliny the Elder. Natural History. A Selection*. Harmondsworth: Penguin Books, 1991

Henderson, John *The Roman Book of Gardening*. London: Routledge, 2004

Hobhouse, Penelope *Plants in Garden History*. London: Pavilion, 1992

Hobhouse, Penelope *The Story of Gardening*. London: Dorling Kindersley, 2002

Mattingly, H (trans) *Tacitus. The Agricola and The Germanica*. Harmondsworth: Penguin Books, 1970

Radice, Betty (trans) *The Letters of the Younger Pliny*. Harmondsworth: Penguin Books, 1969

Ryley, Claire *Roman Gardens and their Plants*. Lewes: Sussex Archaeological Society, 1998

Turner, Tom *Garden History: Philosophy and Design, 2000 BC–2000 AD*. London: Spon Press, 2005

Uglow, Jennifer *A Little History of British Gardening*. London: Chatto & Windus, 2004

Whiteman, Yvonne (ed) *A Garden of Latin Verse*. London: Frances Lincoln, 1998

Wilkinson, Alix *The Garden in Ancient Egypt*. London: Rubicon Press, 1998

Many common features used in gardens today, such as this pergola, were also used in ancient Roman gardens

Useful organisations and societies

The Museum of Garden History

The Museum of Garden History exists to enhance understanding and appreciation of the history and development of gardens and gardening in the UK, and was the world's first museum dedicated to this subject. Its attractions include a recreated 17th-century knot garden with historically authentic planting and collections of tools and gardening ephemera, as well as a well-stocked library.

www.museumgardenhistory.org

The Royal Horticultural Society

The RHS is the world's leading horticultural organisation and the UK's leading gardening charity dedicated to advancing horticulture and promoting good gardening. It offers free horticultural advice and a seed service for its members and has plant centres at its four flagship gardens.

www.rhs.org.uk

The Garden History Society

The Garden History Society aims to promote the study of the history of gardening, landscape gardens and horticulture, and to promote the protection and conservation of historic parks, gardens and designed landscapes and advise on their restoration. The Society runs a series of lectures, tours and events throughout the year.

www.gardenhistorysociety.org

The National Council for the Conservation of Plants and Gardens

The NCCPG seeks to conserve, document, promote and make available Britain and Ireland's garden plants for the benefit of horticulture, education and science. Its National Plant Collection scheme has 630 National Collections held in trust by private owners, specialist growers, arboreta, colleges, universities and botanic gardens.

www.nccpg.com

The Henry Doubleday Research Association

HDRA is a registered charity and Europe's largest organic membership organisation. It is dedicated to researching and promoting organic gardening, farming and food. The HDRA's Heritage Seed Library saves hundreds of old and unusual vegetable varieties for posterity, also distributing them to its members. The HDRA currently manages the kitchen garden at Audley End, Essex, for English Heritage and runs Yalding Organic Gardens.

www.hdra.org.uk

Centre for Organic Seed Information

Funded by DEFRA and run by the National Institute of Agricultural Botany and the Soil Association, the Centre for Organic Seed Information is a 'one-stop shop' for sourcing certified-organic seed from listed suppliers. It covers fruits, vegetables, grasses, herbs and ornamental plants among others.

www.cosi.org.uk

Places to visit

Britain

Bignor Roman Villa
Pulborough
West Sussex RH20 1PH
Tel: 01798 869259
E-mail: bignorromanvilla@care4free.net

Birmingham Botanical Gardens and Glasshouses
Westbourne Road
Edgbaston
Birmingham B15 3TR
Tel: 0121 4541860
E-mail: admin@birminghambotanicalgardens.org.uk
www.birminghambotanicalgardens.org.uk

Calleva
Silchester Roman Town
Wall Lane
Silchester
Hampshire
Tel: 0118 9316255
E-mail: a.s.clarke@reading.ac.uk

Chedworth Roman Villa
Yanworth
Nr Cheltenham
Gloucestershire GL54 3LJ
Tel: 01242 890256
E-mail: chedworth@nationaltrust.org.uk

Corinium Museum
Park Street
Cirencester
Gloucesterhsire GL7 2BX
Tel: 01285 655611
E-mail: museums@cotswold.gov.uk

Fishbourne Roman Palace
Salthill Road
Fishbourne
Chichester
West Sussex PO19 3QS
Tel: 01243 785859
E-mail: adminfish@sussexpast.co.uk

Lullingstone Roman Villa
Eynsford
Kent
DA4 0JA
Tel: 01322 863467
www.english-heritage.org.uk

Verulamium Museum
St Michael's Street
St Albans
Hertfordshire AL3 4SW
Tel: 01727 751810
E-mail: museums@stalbans.gov.uk

Vindolanda
Chesterholm Museum
Bardon Mill
Hexham
Northumberland NE47 7JN
Tel: 01434 344277
E-mail: info@vindolanda.com
www.vindolanda.com

International

Pompeii
Piazza Anfiteatro
Campania
Italy
Tel: +39 081 857 5331

Herculaneum Roman Town
Piazzo Museo
Corso Resina
Ercolano (NA)
Italy
Tel: +39 081 788 1243

Villa Adriana (Hadrian's Villa)
Tivoli
Lazio
Italy
E-mail: info@villa-adriana.net

J Paul Getty Museum and Garden
1200 Getty Center Drive
Los Angeles, CA 90049-1679
USA
Tel: +1 (310) 440 7330
E-mail: gettymuseum@getty.edu
www.getty.edu

Acknowledgements and picture credits

English Heritage and the Museum of Garden History would like to thank the many individuals who contributed to this volume, in particular Rowan Blaik for technical editing, James O Davies for photography and Dr John Pearce and Gill Campbell for their helpful comments on the manuscript. Thanks to the Royal Botanic Gardens Kew for allowing access to the gardens for photography.

The author would like to acknowledge the invaluable assistance of Jane Wilson, Fiona Hope and Philip Norman at the Museum of Garden History.

Unless otherwise stated images are © English Heritage. All English Heritage photographs taken by James Davies, except 2, 7 (John Critchley), 8 (Jonathan Bailey) and 40 (Nigel Corrie). Original artwork by Judith Dobie.

Other illustrations reproduced by kind permission of:

akg-images, London: fc, 60 (Erich Lessing); © The Bodleian Library, University of Oxford: 58 (MS. Bodl. 130, fol. 35v), 65 (MS. Bodl. 130, fol. 4v); Keith Branigan: 52; Bridgeman Art Library: 12 (Temple of Hephaestus, Athens, Greece, Index), 16 (British Museum, London, UK); 18 (Palace of the Alhambra, Granada, Spain, Ken Welsh), 37 (© Ashmolean Museum, University of Oxford, UK), 41b (Hadrian's Villa, Tivoli, Italy), 57 (Biblioteca Marciana, Venice, Italy, Giraudon), 66t (Musée du Bardo, Tunis, Tunisia); © Copyright the Trustees of the British Museum: 62; Maureen Carroll: 31, 32l, 34, 66b; © English Heritage.NMR: 48; Fishbourne Roman Palace/Sussex Archaeological Society: 49, 50, 51; Damian Grady: 22b, 25; Anne Jennings: 14, 22t, 33t, 46; Library of Congress, Prints & Photographs Division, Photochrom Collection LC-DIG-ppmsc-06585: 32r; Mary Evans Picture Library: 19, 24r, 36, 41t; © Crown copyright.NMR: 53, 78; Photo Scala, Florence: 13, 20, 23, 24l, 29, 33b, 67; René Rodgers: 59; Skyscan Balloon Photography: 3; Fiona Small: bc, 27.

Every effort has been made to trace copyright holders and we apologise in advance for any unintentional omissions or errors, which we would be pleased to correct in any subsequent edition of the book.

About the author

Anne Jennings is a freelance garden designer, consultant and writer, and Head of Horticulture at the Museum of Garden History. She is the co-author of *Knot Gardens and Parterres*, published by Barn Elms, and writes for a variety of gardening magazines.

Other titles in this series